explⒶre...

The Forest of
Nisene Marks
State Park

by Jeff Thomson

Walkabout
Publications

Published by
Walkabout Publications
P.O. Box 1299
Soquel, CA 95073
(408) 462-3370

Text Copyright © 1995 by Jeff Thomson
FIRST EDITION 1995
Printed in the United States
of America on recycled paper

Design – Bert J. Ihlenfeld & Associates
Inside Front Cover Photo – Jeff Thomson
Maps – Patrick Santana
Illustrations – Anne Scott

Maps Copyright © 1995 Walkabout Publications. Illustrations remain property of the original copyright holder. All photos are used by permission.

ISBN Number 0-9636945-2-9
Library of Congress Catalog Card
Number 95-90172

This book is dedicated to the Advocates For Nisene Marks State Park.

Acknowledgements

I want to thank the people who made this book possible.

First, I want to thank my wife Debbie. Without her patience and unfailing support this book would not have been possible. Jeff Hicks provided inspiration for the project and gave invaluable assistance through every phase of the book's development. Park ranger, Jerry Waggoner, was always available to answer questions and provide resource information. Extra special assistance came from Ron Powell who allowed me unlimited access to his voluminous historical research and photo collection. Kent Devereaux and Woods Mattingley were also very kind to share their historical research. Fellow members of the Advocates For Nisene Marks State Park, Jeff and Judy Alexander, Alice Harper and Jim Nee gave much needed technical assistance. Also, geologist, Jerry Weber, graciously volunteered to write about the Loma Prieta earthquake and park geology. Many thanks to my conscientious friends who reviewed the manuscript as it progressed and who helped bring order to the book. I am extremely grateful to Lisa Locklin who spent many hours patiently typing multiple revisions of the manuscript. I would also like to thank Kit Salisbury, Margaret Hicks, Rick Hamman, the UCSC Special Collections Room, Santa Cruz County Historical Trust and Pajaro Valley Historical Association.

I am indebted to all these fine people.

Table of Contents

Introduction   1
For Your Information   3
Park Regulations   6
History   7
Points of Interest   11
Geology   16
Wildlife   20
Trees & Plants   22
The Trails   27
- Aptos Creek Road/Fire Road   30
- Aptos Creek Trail   36
- Aptos Rancho Trail   40
- Big Slide Trail   42
- Bridge Creek Trail   43
- Buggy Trail   45
- Hinckley Fire Road   46
- Loma Prieta Grade Trail   49
- Mill Pond Trail   55
- Porter Trail   56
- Split Stuff Trail   57
- Terrace Trail   58
- Trout Gulch Trail   60
- Vienna Woods Trail   61
- West Ridge Trail   63
- Whites Lagoon Trail   66
Index   67
How You Can Help the Park   68
Park Maps   Inside Back Cover

introduction

Tucked away in the coastal mountains of central Santa Cruz County is one of the hidden treasures of the California state park system, the Forest of Nisene Marks. Covered with second-growth redwood trees, the park's 10,000 acres are a labyrinth of cool creek canyons and steep mountain ridges that seem to run helter-skelter in all directions. Over 40 miles of fire roads and trails lace the park making it a haven for hikers, runners, mountain bike enthusiasts and equestrians.

The park's rugged topography is partially the result of earthquakes which have gradually raised the mountains over millions of years. The San Andreas fault skirts the northern boundary while the Zayante fault slices diagonally through the center of the park. The epicenter area of the 1989 Loma Prieta earthquake, which registered 7.1 on the Richter scale, is located about 5 miles from the park entrance.

While earthquakes raise the mountains, stream erosion slowly grinds them down. Starting near Santa Rosalia Ridge at the park's upper boundary, Aptos and Hinckley creeks cut through the mountains on their path to the sea. Aptos Creek rises to the surface at an elevation of 2500 feet then sets a course through the center of the park where it joins another perennial stream, Bridge Creek. From its headwaters, Hinckley Creek drops 2200 feet in only 4.5 miles on a twisting path before joining Soquel Creek along the park's western edge.

The land that now constitutes the park was once covered with immense old-growth redwood trees that were up to 1000 years old. In 1883 a railroad was pushed up Aptos Creek Canyon which provided commercial lumber interests access to some of the best stands of uncut redwood timber south of San Francisco. Soon, sawmills and logging camps sprang up and the redwood giants began to fall. By 1923 the land was virtually stripped bare of its old-growth redwood trees. With nothing left to cut, the loggers pulled out and the forest began to heal. Over the years, young trees have reclaimed the land and obscured much of the evidence of the logging era. Today, as you travel through the park, it is difficult to imagine the sight of trains chugging through the canyons, the sounds of ax and saw and the thunder of timber crashing to earth.

Most of the property within the park boundary was purchased in the 1950s by the Marks family of the Salinas Valley. With the assistance of the Nature Conservancy, they deeded the land to the State of California in 1963 in memory of the family matriarch, Nisene, an ardent lover of nature. The donation was made with the stipulation that the property be left undeveloped. Today, the Forest of Nisene Marks offers you the opportunity to explore a slice of Santa Cruz County history and experience miles of trails in a serene, natural setting just minutes from the rush of civilization.

for your information

The Forest of Nisene Marks State Park is open all year from 6:00 am to sunset. There is an entrance fee.

Getting to the Park

The main entrance to the park is located on Aptos Creek Road in Aptos Village, 7 miles south of the city of Santa Cruz. To reach the main entrance, exit Highway 1 at the Seacliff Beach off ramp. Then drive inland about one block on State Park Drive to Soquel Drive. After turning right on Soquel Drive, you will reach the intersection with Aptos Creek Road in about one-half mile.

The park is also accessible by foot or bicycle from the locations listed below:

From Aptos Rancho Road: Aptos Rancho Road intersects with Soquel Drive at the stoplight across from Rancho Del Mar Shopping Center.

From Vienna Woods Area: From Soquel Drive in Aptos turn on Vienna Drive. Turn left on Wilshire, then right on Danube. The Vienna Woods Trail is just beyond the end of the pavement.

From the North: The Aptos Creek Fire Road along the park's northern boundary can be reached by the following routes:

- Summit Road to Highland Way to Buzzard Lagoon Road
- Eureka Canyon Road to Buzzard Lagoon Road
- Eureka Canyon Road to Rider Road to Buzzard Lagoon Road

Note: To reach the upper locked gate on the fire road requires driving on unpaved roads. During periods of wet weather the roads may be impassable. Parking is limited to several pullouts along the road.

From Soquel Demonstration State Forest: The Soquel Demonstration State Forest shares a common boundary with the Forest of Nisene Marks State Park along Santa Rosalia Ridge. The upper portion of Aptos Creek Fire Road can be reached by taking the Corral Trail in the Soquel Demonstration State Forest. The entrance to the forest is located 6 miles east of Soquel-San Jose Road (Old San Jose Road) on Highland Way.

From the West (Olive Springs Road): From Old San Jose Road turn on to Olive Springs Road and go about 1.2 miles. The unmarked fire road into the park is accessible at an unsigned, locked metal gate across the street from a weigh station building. Parking is limited to a few pullouts along the road. The fire road goes through private property on a right-of-way for about 0.5 miles until it reaches the park boundary sign. Please respect the private property as you pass through.

> *Note: To enter or exit the park at this location requires 4 unbridged creek crossings. This may be difficult or dangerous especially during or after periods of rain.*

Weather

The park enjoys a temperate climate because of its close proximity to the Pacific Ocean. Coastal fog is common between May and August. Summer temperatures range from 50°-60° in the morning rising to 70°-90° by mid-afternoon. The upper regions of the park have open, exposed areas which may get especially warm.

The rainy season generally occurs from mid-November to April with January and February being the wettest months.

Camping

Overnight camping is allowed only at the West Ridge Trail Camp and requires an advance reservation. There is a fee of $7 per night per campsite.

The trail camp consists of six campsites and a restroom. No water is available so you will need to bring your own. Only backpacking stoves are allowed. Overnight parking is at West Ridge Trailhead or George's Picnic Area depending on weather conditions and the time of year. Call (408) 761-3487 for reservations.

Picnic Areas

The park provides three picnic areas furnished with tables, barbecue grills, and restroom facilities. All are located along Aptos Creek Road in picturesque settings near the creek.

George's Picnic Area: Named after an avid outdoorsman who had a special affection for this sunny site. It is located 1 mile from the entrance station near the first bridge crossing Aptos Creek. Facilities include four picnic tables, raised barbecue grills and a restroom. A pay telephone is located across the nearby bridge over Aptos Creek.

Mary Easton Picnic Area: Mary Easton was the wife of Warren Porter, who was secretary of the Loma Prieta Lumber Company and later became Lieutenant Governor of the State of California. This picnic area is the largest in the park with seven picnic sites that include tables and raised barbecue grills. It is located 1.5 miles from the park's entrance station, in a grove of redwood trees, along Aptos Creek Road.

Porter Family Picnic Area: Located about 2.2 miles from the entrance station, this attractive picnic site is situated down in the canyon next to Aptos Creek and has three picnic tables with barbecue grills. The site is named after the Porter family who played an influential role in the lumber company and its operation.

From 1901-1904, the parking area was the site of a small logging camp known as Shillings Camp. It consisted of cabins to house the workers, a barn to store hay and bed down the mules, a blacksmith shop and cookhouse.

Shillings Camp – now the Porter Family Picnic Area parking lot.
Courtesy: California State Library, Sacramento, California

park regulations

The following regulations are intended to enhance your enjoyment of the park and to protect its resources:

Park Hours: The park is open all year from 6:00 am to sunset.

Motor Vehicles: Restricted to Aptos Creek Road and parking areas. Vehicles are not permitted beyond the locked gate at the Porter Family Picnic Area. Overnight parking is not allowed except for registered backpackers. The speed limit in the park is 15 miles per hour.

Dogs: Welcome on Aptos Creek Road and in the picnic areas. Dogs are not allowed on the road beyond the Porter Family Picnic Area. They must be on a leash at all times. Park regulations require that leashes be no longer than 6 feet.

Firearms: Not permitted in the park.

Plants, Animals and Historic Objects: Protected by law. Please do not disturb or remove these features.

Fires: Permitted only in the charcoal grills in the picnic areas. Backpackers using West Ridge Trail Camp should use backpack stoves. Campfires are not permitted.

Smoking: Permitted only in the picnic areas and parking lots.

Fishing: Fishing for steelhead is allowed *below* the first bridge crossing Aptos Creek and only during the open winter season. A valid California fishing license is required.

Private Property: Some trails pass near or briefly through private property. Please respect the park's neighbors and their right to privacy.

Equestrian Use: Horses are permitted on most trails below the first bridge crossing Aptos Creek.

Bicycle Use: *Above* the first bridge crossing Aptos Creek, bicyclists are restricted to the fire roads. Violators can be cited and fined. *Below the first bridge*, bicyclists may use all of the trails except the Buggy Trail. Policy regarding bicycle use of park trails is subject to change. Bikes going downhill:

- Go slowly (the speed limit is 15 mph).
- Ride single file.
- Watch for other park users.

history

The "Disappearing" History of Nisene Marks State Park

At first glance, the Forest of Nisene Marks State Park may appear to be a primeval forest untouched by civilization. In reality, this area was a beehive of activity during an intensive 40 year logging frenzy (1883-1923). The estimated 140 million board feet of lumber that were removed from the forest, would, if loaded onto railroad flatcars, stretch a distance of almost 39 miles! While much evidence of the logging era has disappeared, the alert visitor can still find clues that stir the imagination and provide a window into this colorful chapter in Santa Cruz County history.

Our story begins...

During the Mexican period of California history (1822-1848), land grants were awarded to loyal Mexican citizens, many of whom were "Californios"– Hispanic people born in California before it became a state. In 1833 Martina Castro, a Californio living near Santa Cruz, obtained a 1668 acre land grant named Rancho Soquel. In 1844 most of the land that now constitutes the state park, was awarded to Martina Castro in another land grant called the Rancho Soquel Augmentation. Consisting of 32,700 acres, it was the largest land grant in the Santa Cruz region.

Following the gold rush of 1849, California experienced a tidal wave of immigration which quadrupled the state's population by 1860. This influx of people caused an increasing demand for building products, especially lumber from the redwood tree, prized for its straight grain and durability. In their search for "red gold," the loggers focused on the Castro property in Aptos Creek Canyon, which was believed to hold some of the best stands of uncut redwood timber south of San Francisco.

In early 1883 the Loma Prieta Lumber Company purchased 6845 acres from Carmel Fallon, a daughter of Martina Castro. That land, now within the current park boundary, included the coveted timber in Aptos Creek Canyon. The problem then faced by the lumber company was how to find a practical and profitable way to get their new timber to market. The best solution was to build a railroad into the steep and winding canyon, but that would require a financial outlay far beyond their means. In short order, financial backing was obtained from the Southern Pacific Railroad Company and one of the most extensive logging operations to ever take place in Santa Cruz County would soon begin.

Timber!

By the summer of 1883 the Southern Pacific Railroad Company began constructing a railroad that would extend seven miles up Aptos Creek Canyon from the main line in Aptos Village. Over the next 40 years, spur lines would be pushed up almost every canyon and more than five miles of narrow-gauge (30 inch) railroad would be built in the upper regions of the park.

During the logging era, several temporary logging camps were constructed along with one small town, Loma Prieta. Established in the mid 1880s, Loma Prieta was not a typical logging camp with ramshackle cabins. Instead, it consisted of comfortable buildings suitable for families and at its peak boasted a population of about 300. The Southern Pacific Railroad Company promoted the town as a tourist destination as did local newspapers. Periodicals of the day advertised the Loma Prieta area as "a new and charming retreat for tourists, pleasure seekers and campers." Located about 3.5 miles above Aptos Village along the present day Aptos Creek Fire Road, the town included a sawmill, railroad station, post office, Wells Fargo tele-

Loma Prieta Sawmill and storage yard with houses for millworkers.
Courtesy: Special Collections University Library UCSC

graph office, saloon, company store, a small hotel and a one-room schoolhouse. In addition, there were houses for logging company directors and employees.

Even though the town of Loma Prieta offered some degree of comfort, the loggers' work schedule provided little time for recreation. Work days lasted 11 hours, six days a week. They started work at 6:00 am, took 50 minutes for lunch (instead of the standard 60 minutes), then labored until the 6:00 pm whistle. On Saturday, the crew ended the day early at 5:00 pm having made up the extra hour with shorter lunch breaks during the week.

In addition to logs sent down to the mill, redwood trees were often cut and processed where they fell into "split stuff" (grape stakes, firewood, fence posts, etc.), which was usually carried out to the railroad line by mules. In some places where the terrain was too steep even for the mules, overhead cables (up to a mile in length) were installed to get the cut wood out. Today, stacks of split stuff left behind by the loggers can still be found in a few remote areas of the park.

By 1923, the lumber company had pretty much exhausted the supply of old-growth redwoods. They sold off what equipment and buildings they could and abandoned the rest. Over the years much of what they left behind has been obscured by a tangle of bushes and vines, buried under landslides or washed away by violent winter storms. In short, most of the evidence from the logging era has disappeared. However, by understanding what took place here and searching for "clues," the disappearing history of the park will come alive.

Since many of today's hiking trails follow the old railroad grades, you may still see wooden crossties, metal spikes and the occasional rusting rail. Wire cables used to pull the logs are also scattered about. Other clues to the park's history can be found in some of the creekbeds in the form of wooden train trestle timbers. At some of the old logging camp sites, dilapidated cabins and housing foundations are still evident. Also, places where the loggers lived are sometimes marked by non-native plants such as ivy and periwinkle. In the upper regions of the park, stacks of cut wood can still be found along with downed logs that were never removed. Perhaps the most common and lasting evidence of the logging era is the springboard notch. Throughout the park almost every tree stump has a springboard notch – a small square cut into the side of the stump into which a board was placed to build a raised platform on which the loggers stood while cutting the tree. The platform was built to get above the tree's butt swell, since that wood was twisted and hard to cut.

Two loggers standing on platform supported by springboards.
Courtesy: California Department of Parks & Recreation

Establishing the Park

There had been speculation since the turn of the century that there was oil to be found in the Santa Cruz Mountains. It was this search for black gold that prompted Herman Marks, his sister Agnes and brother Andrew, to purchase 9700 acres from the lumber companies (and other private property owners) from 1951-1953. However, the Marks' drilling efforts never produced a drop of oil. In 1963, through the assistance of the Nature Conservancy, the Marks family deeded 9700 acres to the State of California in memory of their mother, Nisene. With the further assistance of the Save-the-Redwood League, additional properties were purchased along lower Aptos Creek to bring the total park size to 10,036 acres.

points of interest

First Bridge Crossing Aptos Creek

From the bridge located near George's Picnic Area, you are provided with a picturesque view of Aptos Creek as it winds through a narrow canyon.

Loma Prieta Mill Site

The Loma Prieta Sawmill operated from the mid 1880s to the early 1920s. Today, all that remains of the mill are its foundation timbers.

Loma Prieta Sawmill circa mid 1890s.
Courtesy: Special Collections University Library UCSC

A town called Loma Prieta was established in the area surrounding the mill growing to a population of about 300 people. Although it has vanished, almost without a trace, Loma Prieta once boasted a post office, hotel, saloon, company store, offices for both Western

Coates Saloon and the first Loma Prieta hotel.
Courtesy:
Pajaro Valley Historical Association

Union and Wells Fargo telegraph plus facilities for the local telephone company. It also had a large, one-room building that served as a schoolhouse during the day, a meeting hall at night and as the village church on Sundays.

As the town grew in size, so did its reputation as a recreation center. A dance hall, picnic areas and campground were added to attract visitors. Local newspapers extolled the advantages of vacationing in the area.

Porter House Site

Warren Porter was the secretary for the Loma Prieta Lumber Company and lived in a comfortable house with his wife Mary Easton and son John. Warren Porter later became Lieutenant Governor of the State of California.

The Porter House.
Courtesy: Santa Cruz County Historical Trust

This site is also the location of a building that served as the directors' cottage. It contained seven bedrooms, one for each member of the lumber company's board of directors, who would stay here while conducting their monthly meetings.

Hoffman's Historic Site

This logging camp was used from 1918-1921, during the last major logging effort in the park. Named after camp superintendent, Louis Hoffman and his wife the camp cook, it consisted of about 25 buildings plus a 120-foot long bunkhouse with adjoining showers and washrooms. The camp also included the cookhouse with living quarters for the Hoffmans, a meeting hall, corrals and barns for the mules, a blacksmith shop and several cabins built by men who did not want

to live in the bunkhouse. This camp is the best "preserved" historic site in the park with the remains of several dilapidated cabins scattered throughout the general area.

The Hoffmans.
Courtesy: Santa Cruz County
Historical Trust

Bridge Creek Historic Site

This small logging camp was used from 1917-1918 and consisted of several shanties built along Bridge Creek. The remains of the camp were washed downstream during a major storm in 1982, leaving only a pile of old boards that now mark the site.

Maple Falls

A 30-foot waterfall located about 0.5 miles upstream from the Bridge Creek Historic Site. Bridge Creek flows all year, but during the dry months, it is possible to walk up the creekbed to see the waterfall.

Earthquake Epicenter Area

This location along Aptos Creek is near the epicenter of the 1989 Loma Prieta earthquake, which registered 7.1 on the Richter scale.

Bottom of the Incline

The incline was a short but steep section of narrow-gauge (30 inch) railroad line. It was built in 1912 by the Molino Timber Company to transport "split stuff" (grape stakes, shingles, posts) down from their logging operations in the upper regions of today's park. The rise in elevation from bottom to top was about 600 feet over a distance of 2250 feet, too steep for a train engine to operate. Instead, railcars were lowered down the hill using wire cable attached to a spool on a steam donkey. A steam donkey was a wood-fired boiler mounted on a movable wooden sled. This machine, which generated enough steam power to pull redwood logs, used a system of gears and cables attached to large drums. When the steam donkey needed to be moved, the cables were attached to a sturdy tree and the donkey dragged itself to its new location.

The bottom of the incline was located just above and to the right of the footbridge that crosses Aptos Creek, near the earthquake epicenter area sign.

Top of the Incline

It was at this location on the Aptos Creek Fire Road that the Molino Timber Company loaded stacks of split wood on narrow-gauge railcars and lowered them down the steep slope using wire cable attached to a steam donkey. The facilities here included a small train switchyard, repair shop and blacksmith shop.

Workers posing at the Top of the Incline.
Courtesy: California Department of Parks & Recreation

Whites Lagoon

A small sag pond located in a high meadow, Whites Lagoon depends on winter rain for its water. It sustains a variety of wildlife and is considered an ecologically sensitive area.

Another pond, Buzzard Lagoon, is located in the northeast corner of the park.

Sand Point Overlook

At an elevation of 1600 feet, this spot is considered to be the best viewpoint in the park. On a clear day you can see the city of Santa Cruz, the Pacific Ocean, UC Santa Cruz and the Santa Cruz Mountains as they stretch north toward San Francisco. The Molino Timber Company's narrow-gauge railroad line ran along today's Aptos Creek Fire Road at this location. Also, legend has it that a 10-ton train engine lies buried under tons of debris somewhere below Sand Point.

Camp 2

A small logging camp that was established about 1914 and populated mainly by Japanese workers who produced split wood products for the Molino Timber Company. It is located next to the fire road one mile above Sand Point Overlook. Very little remains of the camp except for a few scattered boards.

Two directors of the Molino Timber Company inspecting split stuff near Camp 2.
Courtesy:
California Department of Parks & Recreation

Lone Tree Prairie

Hardly a small, flat area much less a "prairie," this location can be identified by a large, fire-scarred, old-growth redwood tree on the left side of the fire road 2.5 miles above Sand Point. In this area, the lumber company anchored a mile-long overhead cable which was coupled to a steam donkey engine to lift split wood products out of the steep and deep Hinckley Basin.

geology

The Loma Prieta Earthquake in the Forest of Nisene Marks State Park

Gerald E. Weber

At 5:15 pm on October 17, 1989, twelve miles below China Ridge in the Forest of Nisene Marks, the North American Plate and the Pacific Plate suddenly shifted ever so slightly. As the two huge plates slid past each other, the fault rupture propagated northwestward through the crust like an opening zipper. The fault rupture also moved upward, toward the surface, along the southward-tilted fault, but died out before reaching the surface. Radiating outward from the initial point of rupture, an expanding spherical wave front reached the surface in eight seconds. Fifteen seconds of violent shaking later, it was all over. The Forest of Nisene Marks was changed permanently, having moved slightly (4 feet) northwest and also slightly higher (20 inches), in respect to North America. The greatest uplift occurred in the north end of the park resulting in a slight but imperceptible tilt of the area to the southwest.

To local residents the Loma Prieta earthquake was an uncommon and unanticipated event, but geologically, such events are common. Similar earthquakes slowly raised the Santa Cruz Mountains in a series of small jumps over millions of years and the uplift continues. As mountains are raised by earthquakes, stream erosion and landslides slowly grind them down. Streams continue to erode their courses across the rising mountains, while landslides crash into the canyons, waiting to be carried to the sea by the streams they dam. It is this dynamic interplay between earthquake generated uplift and gravity driven landsliding and stream erosion, that has formed the rugged topography in the park.

The deep, rugged and steep walled canyons of Aptos, Bridge and Hinckley creeks result from rapid down cutting by swift moving streams with steep gradients. They are the sign of a youthful landscape, in which streams struggle to lower their beds as rapidly as the mountains are uplifted by earthquakes. They are in an ideal setting for landslides masses of weathered and broken rock and soil that break loose on slopes and move down slope under the force of gravity.

Landslides are a common event; some occur almost every year in which rainfall is sufficient to saturate soils and weathered rock. To the hiker or visitor, most of these slides go unnoticed. It is the infrequent earthquake or heavy rainfall that triggers many landslides that is noticed by the visiting public.

To a hiker, the violent shaking of the 1989 earthquake created havoc. Downed trees, cracked ground and large landslides damaged trails and blocked streams. Lateral forces snapped the tops off of redwood trees, littering the forest floor with treetops. Shallow soil slides, debris avalanches, rock falls and landslides denuded 0.7 miles of the steep inner canyon wall of Aptos Creek east of Whites Lagoon. Small landslides were common along the steep inner gorge of Hinckley Creek and narrow ridge crests were often shattered in a complex web of ground cracks. This instantaneous transformation of the landscape captures the eye. Yet, such episodes are often separated by time periods longer than most human lifetimes. Hence, earthquakes or other catastrophic events seem to be the dominant forces shaping the landscape, when in reality, the slow and steady, but nearly imperceptible forces of rain, weathering and stream erosion are doing most of the work.

Although damage due to landslides appeared severe, the effects of the Loma Prieta earthquake were relatively minor compared to what is typical during large earthquakes. Fragmentary and incomplete data from the great earthquake on April 18, 1906 suggest that landsliding in the Forest of Nisene Marks during that earthquake was similar if not greater than that which occurred in 1989. The Hinckley Creek landslide of April 18, 1906 that buried the Loma Prieta Mill and killed nine men had no equal during 1989. The probable reasons for more landsliding in 1906 include a longer duration of shaking and significantly greater soil moisture, since the 1906 earthquake occurred following a rainy winter. The Loma Prieta earthquake occurred at the end of a long, dry summer following three drought years.

Detailed geological mapping of landslides following the 1989 earthquake revealed over a thousand landslides within the park. However, the vast majority of these slides are old and probably were not triggered by seismic shaking. Rather, they are thought to have originated during periods of unusually high rainfall due to the changed climate of the last ice age, between 15,000 and 30,000 years ago.

Although the clear-cutting of saleable redwoods during the logging frenzy (1883-1923) stripped most of the hillsides in the park, there is no evidence that logging led to an episode of increased landsliding. Some landslides are clearly related to logging, but the number appears to be small.

FAULT ZONES

The San Andreas fault zone, the primary fault within the greater San Andreas fault system, dominates California geology. The fault lies immediately north of the park boundary. Corralitos Creek and the east branch of Soquel Creek have both eroded their linear courses along the easily eroded rocks of the San Andreas fault zone. In the Santa Cruz Mountains (as elsewhere) the San Andreas fault zone is most often expressed as a linear canyon.

The San Andreas fault zone is the main break in a wide complex system of faults that form the boundary between two immense crustal plates that slowly and inexorably slide past each other at a rate of about one to two inches per year. East of the fault lies all of North America and the west half of the Atlantic Ocean (North American Plate). West of the fault lies coastal California and the floor of the entire Pacific Ocean all the way to Japan (Pacific Plate). As the North American Plate moves to the southeast the Pacific Plate moves northwestward toward the Aleutian Trench. During the past 15-20 million years, the San Andreas fault has displaced rocks some 300-500 miles. Hence, older rocks in the Santa Cruz Mountains are similar to rocks found hundreds of miles to the south on the eastern side of the fault zone.

The Zayante fault is one of many large active branch faults of the San Andreas fault system present in the Santa Cruz Mountains and the San Francisco Bay area. The Zayante fault is an active fault, but it moves much more slowly and intermittently than the San Andreas fault. Earthquakes occur infrequently, separated by long intervals (thousands of years) of inactivity. Average slip rates are thought to be significantly less than an inch per year, with the southwest side of the fault moving to the northwest in respect to the eastern side. The western side has apparently also been raised in respect to the area northeast of the fault.

The Zayante fault crosses the park through Hell's Gate in the Aptos Creek Canyon, but its exact location is a matter of debate. The fault is not obvious nor can it be readily seen in the park. Thick soils, deeply weathered rocks, numerous landslides and dense vegetation make it exceedingly difficult to locate the exact path of the Zayante (or any other) fault through this area.

THE ROCKS

The bedrock geology of the park reflects long years of lateral transport of rock units along the faults of the San Andreas fault system. The southwestern portion of the park is underlain by relatively flat lying sandstones and silty sandstones that were deposited on a shallow ocean floor about 5-8 million years ago. These relatively soft and poorly consolidated sandstones and siltstones of the Purisima Formation are susceptible to landsliding, particularly on steep slopes in the inner gorge of the stream canyons. Most of the landslides that occurred during the Loma Prieta earthquake occurred within these rocks.

Further inland, in the higher regions of the park, the rocks consist of harder, better consolidated and more strongly cemented sandstones and shales. These rocks experienced less landsliding and slippage during the 1989 earthquake than the younger Purisima Formation. The largest, active landslide present in the park formed in these older and harder rocks, apparently in response to heavy rainfalls in the early 1980s.

The recent Loma Prieta earthquake and the slope failure processes triggered by the seismic shaking are part of a continuing cycle of geologic processes that have shaped the park. The geologic history of the Forest of Nisene Marks over the past several million years is dominated by weathering, landsliding of weathered rock and stream erosion. These processes create the landscape by shaping the ridges and deepening and widening the canyons that drain the Santa Cruz Mountains. Intermittent earthquakes raise the mountains, rejuvenating the streams, while seismically triggered landslides strip weathered rock and soil from the hillsides. Landslides clean the rock, exposing it to the beginning of another cycle of weathering that will prepare the rock and soil for eventual transport by landslides to the streams below. Streams carry the sediment to the sea. This cycle of weathering, landsliding and stream erosion occasionally interrupted by earthquakes is the recurring theme of the landscape. The earthquake is the great rejuvenator of the cycle as it raises the coastal mountains, and triggers landslides initiating the cycle. These cycles will continue.

wildlife

The Forest of Nisene Marks contains plentiful and diverse wildlife – including mammals, birds, amphibians and reptiles. Many live far above the ground in the forest canopy, or are creatures that only come out at night. The best chance for seeing the park's characteristically shy wildlife is in the early morning or evening hours.

Mammals

Some of more commonly seen mammals are gray squirrels, chipmunks, cottontail rabbits and blacktail deer. As the small mammals and deer have increased in population, so have their predators. Recently coyotes, gray foxes and a mountain lion have been sighted in the park.

The more elusive nocturnal mammals include raccoons, opossums, skunks and bobcats, whose tracks along the streambeds are often the only indication of their presence.

Another nocturnal mammal, which is rarely seen but deserves special mention, is the wild pig. This cross between the European wild boar (introduced into Monterey County in the mid-1920s) and free-roaming feral swine (released by early settlers) is very prolific. Their presence in the park is clearly noticeable in the rototilled soil along the trails, the result of their search for truffles, worms, acorns and roots. Wild pigs generally run from people, but can be aggressive if they are sick or feel threatened.

Reptiles and Amphibians

The three major creeks in the park – Aptos, Bridge, and Hinckley – generally run all year and provide habitat for a variety of small amphibians. Most often seen are the Pacific giant salamander and California slender salamander. Also, the California newt is frequently seen in the wet months, striding across the forest

California Newt

floor or swimming in streams. Moist places under redwood trees provide a perfect habitat for these fragile-skinned animals.

Among the reptiles, the red-legged frog and Pacific tree frog are common along streams, marshy areas and ponds.

Hiking through the park you may encounter an occasional snake, most probably a garter snake or rubber boa – both harmless. The western rattlesnake is the only potentially dangerous reptile in the park. Fortunately, its nocturnal habits rarely bring it in contact with human visitors.

Common lizards in the park include the alligator lizard, western bluetailed skink and the western fence lizard. In the dry chaparral areas, the western fence lizard can be briefly glimpsed scurrying for cover or doing "push-ups" as a territorial gesture.

Birds

While redwood forests are not usually famous for birds, the Forest of Nisene Marks has more than a few. Two of the larger birds are the great horned owl and the redtail hawk. Also, ravens can be heard cawing above the trees.

The most frequently seen bird is the raucous-voiced Stellar's jay. Its cousin, the scrub jay is more common in the upper regions of the park. Also plentiful are the Oregon junco, acorn woodpecker, California quail and the bandtailed pigeon. Brown creepers, nuthatches, and bushtits can be observed as they work their way up and down tree trunks.

Stellar's Jay

The water dipper or water ouzel is a seldom seen but fascinating resident of the creek areas. This chubby wren-sized bird uses its wings to "fly underwater" while hunting aquatic insects.

Also, keep a sharp eye out for the kingfisher as it flies along the creek corridors, and the winter wren which nests along Aptos Creek.

Invertebrates

One of the most popular and colorful invertebrates in the park is the humble banana slug. This bright yellow gastropod can be easily observed in nearly any area of the redwood forest, slowly inching its way across the forest floor.

Banana Slug

trees & plants

The forest is made up of three vegetation communities that vary with the elevation. In the cool, moist canyons at the lower elevations, the redwood forest, including the creekside riparian community, dominates. It gives way to the mixed evergreen forest which in turn gives way at the upper elevations (above 1800 feet) to bristling chaparral along the hot, exposed mountain ridges. Before the forest was logged, these vegetation communities were probably well-defined. Now, while the forest regenerates, their boundaries are blurred and will remain that way for some time until the second-growth redwoods reestablish their dominance.

The Redwood Forest

Prior to 1880, the redwood trees that grew on what is now state park property were majestic old-growth specimens, perhaps up to 1500 years of age. Then the loggers came. When they left 40 years later, the land was charred, creeks ran muddy, and only a few of the ancient giants remained. However, today 20%-30% more redwood trees are growing in the park than before the logging era – testimony to the redwood's prolific power of regeneration.

The coast redwood *(Sequoia sempervirens)* is the dominant tree in the Forest of Nisene Marks State Park. It is the world's tallest tree and also one of the most ancient. Genetically it dates back millions of years to the time of the dinosaurs. Because of dramatic changes in climate and geology these "living fossils," which once covered much of the North American continent, have retreated to a 500-mile long strip of land from southwest Oregon in the north to the Santa Lucia Mountains near Carmel, California, in the south. Their zone of growth is also narrow, only about 30 miles wide and corresponds with the coastal fog belt.

The coast redwood grows in a narrow zone along the California coast and southwestern Oregon.

The redwood's longevity is aided by its bark, which can be up to a foot thick, providing a high degree of fireproofing. Also, a reddish tannic acid permeates the bark and heartwood and affords a high level of resistance to the invasion of insects, bacteria and fungi. Logs can last a hundred years after the death of the tree and the wood in the trunk will often be as fresh as the day it fell.

The reproductive capabilities of the coastal redwood are also quite remarkable. These giants grow from tiny seeds that each mature tree drops by the millions every fall. Most trees, however, come from sprouting stump roots lying near the surface of the soil.

Unlike most trees, the redwood has no tap root. Instead, it develops a tangle of shallow roots that form a pedestal-like base 8 to 12 feet deep and 60 to 80 feet wide. If the parent tree is harmed by fire or

The roots of a redwood are shallow and spread out to capture rain and fog drip.

saw, a ring of new sprouts explodes from its roots toward the sunlight. These sprouts have an advantage over trees that grow from seeds, since they have the parent's root system to feed them.

The ring of new trees that develops around the base of an old tree or stump is often referred to as a "family circle." The trees in the circle are not separate individuals, but a single individual connected at the living root of the mother tree. In the Forest of Nisene Marks, the average family circle may contain 20 to 50 trees of varying ages. As the strongest and most rapidly growing win the competition for sunlight, the number of trees in the circle gradually diminishes over the years until only one or two of them reach old age. The trees you see today in the park are relatively young, 70 to 100 years old, and have not grown tall enough to shade out competitors.

Within the state park, only a few small groves of old-growth redwood trees escaped the logger's ax and saw. One survivor is the Van Eck Tree which is located on Aptos Creek Road near the park entrance. This tree, which is probably close to 1000 years old, was spared by the loggers due to the large number of burls near the base which made it difficult to cut.

The redwoods are most predominate in the moist areas near streams and on the uneven slopes of the upper canyons. They share space along the creek banks with big leaf maple, red alders, California sycamores and thickets of shrub-like red and yellow willows.

The damp redwood forest floor is made up of shade-tolerant plants including a wide variety of ferns. Because of the broad elevation range and varied habitats in the forest, the park boasts of at least 17 different types of ferns.

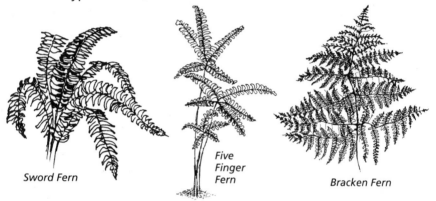

Sword Fern

Five
Finger
Fern

Bracken Fern

In the springtime many varieties of wildflowers show their colors including wild ginger, trillium, wild orchid and redwood sorrel.

The Forest of Nisene Marks State Park is quickly gaining a reputation as a fungus fancier's paradise. In the late fall and early winter, an incredible variety of mushrooms emerge from the forest floor or sprout on rotting logs. As is true with all plants and historical items in the park, mushroom collecting is prohibited.

The Mixed Evergreen Community

If you follow a trail up to an exposed ridge, you will notice the redwood trees soon begin to mix with other evergreen trees such as Douglas fir, tan oak, live oak, California laurel and madrone. The Douglas fir is one of the more common trees in this forest community. This species grows up to 250 feet in height and can be recognized by its long, dark, yellow-green needles and three to four-inch long cones. The Douglas fir is also an important timber species and a popular Christmas tree.

The acorns of the tan oak were an important food source for the

Native Americans (Ohlone) who lived nearby. Later, European settlers prized its bark which was stripped and sent to the city of Santa Cruz where it was used in the local leather tanning industry. Each winter, the madrone tree sheds its bright orange outer bark in papery curls, exposing a smooth, green skin that dries to orange again. The California laurel or bay tree grows in shady places. It produces aromatic leaves which can be dried and used as a seasoning in stews and sauces.

Flowering plants in the mixed evergreen forest are abundant and include two-eyed violet, Douglas iris, flowering currant and false Solomon seal.

The Chaparral Community

The Chaparral community occupies the driest locations along the high south-facing exposed ridgetops (above 1800 feet) and is largely composed of densely growing woody stemmed shrubs such as manzanita, buck brush, coffeeberry and chamise. Taller trees include the California buckeye, knob cone pine and at least three types of oak trees. The pine cones and acorns from these trees provide an important source of food for chaparral wildlife. Common chaparral wildflowers include wild lilac, Indian paintbrush and monkey flower.

Non-Native Plants

During the logging era (1880s-1920s), loggers and their families often planted non-native plants near their homes, such as eucalyptus, black acacia, periwinkle and English ivy. Many of the non-native plants have thrived over the years and block the reestablishment of the native plant species.

Around 1908, the Loma Prieta Lumber Company was giving serious thought to replanting their logged-over lands with fast growing eucalyptus trees. They planted 40-50 acres of eucalyptus and about 200 acacia trees around the Loma Prieta townsite, but due in part to an unseasonably cold winter, most did not survive and the plan was dropped. However, some of these trees still grow in the park and can be seen along the Aptos Creek Fire Road and at the Porter House Site.

In some places, tenacious French broom and stubborn pampas grass have also taken root and there is some effort being made to remove these hardy plants.

Plants to Avoid

Poison Oak flourishes throughout the park. It grows in the form of a bush or vine with leaves in groups of three. In the autumn, the leaves turn red and fall off leaving bare stems. Just by brushing against the leaves or the stems you can pick up its toxic oils and suffer a miserable rash that can last two to three weeks. Learn to identify it.

Stinging Nettle has dark green leaves with saw-toothed edges. The stem and leaves are covered with bristly hairs that, if touched, can inject a stinging irritant.

the trails

The park is laced with over 40 miles of scenic trails providing a variety of options for hikers, bicyclists and equestrians. Some trails lead to historic sites tracing railroad grades built over 100 years ago. Others wind through lush creek canyons or up to viewpoints along mountain ridges. The trails mirror the landscape and range from easy to strenuous, although most fit in the moderate range.

Most of the trailheads are signed and show distances in both miles and kilometers. To help plan your hike, consider that a person in reasonably good physical condition can hike gentle terrain at a pace of 2 to 3 miles per hour. However, steep terrain can slow your pace to as little as one mile per hour. Except for all but the shortest hikes, it is highly recommended that you bring extra water, food and of course a map. Last but not least, remember to slow down and leave yourself extra time to enjoy the sights and sounds of the forest.

Selecting Your Hike

The trails listed in this book are described according to their level of difficulty. Since you are the best judge of your physical condition, these ratings should be used as a general guide.

Easy: *Uneven but fairly level.*
Moderate: *Some steep grades mixed with level stretches.*
Strenuous: *Steep grades, uneven terrain and long steady climbs.*

Limited Time?

Most of the trails below the bridge at George's Picnic Area can be walked in less than two hours.

From the Porter Family Picnic Area, short walks can be made to the Porter House Site, Loma Prieta Mill Site and the earthquake epicenter area.

Practice Trail Etiquette...

- Please be courteous to other trail users.
- Bicyclists should yield to equestrians and hikers; hikers should yield to equestrians.
- Use caution and make your presence known when approaching or overtaking another person.
- To minimize erosion, stay on designated trails.

Please Note: As this book is being developed the earthquake epicenter area sign is being restored and may not be in place upon publication. Also, descriptions of the Aptos Rancho, Split Stuff, Terrace and Vienna Woods trails may refer to signs and markers the park service anticipates having in place by late 1995.

Every attempt has been made to describe the trails as accurately as possible. However, earthquakes, rainstorms and other natural events can significantly change trail conditions. You should not use any of the trails without acknowledging and assuming the risks involved. Please exercise common sense and caution. **You are responsible for determining your own physical ability and for your own safety while using park trails.**

BE AWARE THAT TRAIL CONDITIONS CAN VARY BY SEASON. THERE ARE A NUMBER OF UNBRIDGED STREAM CROSSINGS THAT MAY BE DIFFICULT OR DANGEROUS, ESPECIALLY DURING OR AFTER PERIODS OF RAIN.

Trail Distances
(One Way)

Aptos (Soquel Drive) to:	Miles
Entrance Station	0.8
George's Picnic Area	1.8
West Ridge Trailhead	2.3
Mary Easton Picnic Area	2.4
Porter Family Picnic Area	3.0
Loma Prieta Grade Trailhead	3.2
Loma Prieta Mill Site	3.6
Aptos Creek Trailhead	4.5
Sand Point Overlook	9.0
Soquel Demonstration State Forest Trail	12.4

Aptos Creek Trail to:	
Big Slide Trail	4.0
Five Finger Falls	5.0

Aptos Rancho Trail to:	
Split Stuff Trail	0.7
Terrace Trail	1.1
Vienna Woods Trail	1.3
George's Picnic Area	1.9

Big Slide Trail to:	
Aptos Creek Trail	1.5

Big Stump Gap Trail (from Hoffman's Historic Site) to:	
West Ridge Trail	1.0

Bridge Creek Trail to:	
Bridge Creek Historic Site	1.4

Buggy Trail to:	
Trail's End	0.5

Hinckley Fire Road down to:	
West Ridge Trail Camp	0.4
Park Boundary	3.0
Olive Springs Road	3.5

Loma Prieta Grade Trail to:	Miles
Porter House Site	0.7
Bridge Creek Trail	0.9
Bridge Creek Historic Site	2.3
Hoffman's Historic Site	2.3
Historic Loop	6.0

Mill Pond Trail:	0.1

Porter Trail to:	
Mary Easton or Porter Family Picnic Areas	1.0

Ridge Connection Trail	0.5

Split Stuff Trail to:	
Aptos Rancho Trail	0.2

Terrace Trail to:	
Vienna Woods Trail	0.6
Trail's End	0.9

Trout Gulch Trail to:	
Park Boundary	1.0

Vienna Woods Trail to:	
Terrace Trail	0.4
Trail's End	0.9

West Ridge Trail to:	
Overview Area	5.0
West Ridge Trail Camp	6.0

Whites Lagoon Trail to:	
Big Slide Trail	0.2
Whites Lagoon	0.4

Aptos Creek Road/Fire Road

Starting Point:
Aptos Creek Road at the intersection with Soquel Drive in Aptos

Distances (One Way):
Aptos (Soquel Drive) to:

		Elevation Gain
Entrance station	0.8 miles	
George's Picnic Area	1.8 miles	
Winter gate	2.0 miles	
West Ridge Trailhead	2.3 miles	
Mary Easton Picnic Area	2.4 miles	
Porter Family Picnic Area	3.0 miles	
Loma Prieta Grade Trailhead	3.2 miles	
Loma Prieta Mill Site	3.6 miles	
Aptos Creek Trailhead	4.5 miles	100 feet
Top of the Incline	6.0 miles	760 feet
Whites Lagoon Trail	8.2 miles	1140 feet
Sand Point Overlook	9.0 miles	1400 feet
Soquel Demonstration State Forest Trail	12.4 miles	2300 feet
Santa Rosalia gate	13.3 miles	2200 feet

Classification:
Easy to strenuous

Usage:
(Horses not permitted beyond first bridge crossing Aptos Creek)

HIGHLIGHTS – The Aptos Creek Road/Fire Road travels through the heart of the park and provides access to most of the trails. Sections of this road follow old railroad grades built between 1883 and 1912. It is also possible to reach the Soquel Demonstration State Forest trail system which connects with the fire road 9.4 miles north of the Porter Family Picnic Area.

This road is the most traveled route in the park, at least to the earthquake epicenter area near the Aptos Creek Trailhead. Automobiles are only allowed along the first 3 miles to the Porter Family Picnic Area. Beyond that point travel is by foot or bicycle.

From its intersection with Soquel Drive in Aptos, Aptos Creek Road is paved to the parking area at the entrance station. It passes by one of the few remaining old-growth trees in the park, the Van Eck Tree located next to the park map display. Spared by the loggers because of the large number of burls at its base, this tree is estimated to be about 1000 years old.

Beyond the entrance station, the route is mostly level over the next 2 miles as, for the most part, it traces an old train bed to the locked gate at the Porter Family Picnic Area. Along the way you can access the park's three picnic areas and many of the shorter trails, most of which lead to scenic spots on Aptos Creek.

Past the Porter Family Picnic Area, the road soon reaches the Loma Prieta Grade Trailhead. During the logging era this spot was called Molino. Here the main railroad line curved left up what is now the

Railroad line to the left is today's Loma Prieta Grade Trail. When this photo was taken (about 1885) it was the main line to Loma Prieta. The railroad line to the right leads to a small mill along Aptos Creek. A third line, which was added in the middle, trestled across Aptos Creek and ended at the sawmill. Today's fire road heads directly toward the Molino sign.

Courtesy:
Stanford University Library;
Timothy Hopkins collection

Loma Prieta Grade Trail, while a spur line forked right to a shingle mill on Aptos Creek. Now leaving the railroad bed, the road dips down to the bridge over Aptos Creek. Shortly after crossing the creek, you will enter the area once occupied by the Loma Prieta Lumber Company's storage yard, then quickly arrive at the sawmill site which is marked by a sign. The mill was "fired up" in the mid 1880s and operated on and off through 1922, employing up to 150 workers at its peak. Today, all that remains are some of the mill's foundation timbers.

A town named Loma Prieta was developed in the area around the sawmill with several houses and buildings constructed near what is now the fire road. The town grew to a population of about 300 people and included a railroad station, post office, company store, saloon, hotel and one-room schoolhouse. After the lumber company closed the mill in 1922, many of the remaining buildings were sold to local people who dismantled them and hauled out the lumber. While nothing remains of Loma Prieta, the ivy and periwinkle you see growing along the road were planted by people living in the town and are a clue that a building or homesite was located nearby.

As you continue up the road beyond the mill site, the area on your left was once occupied by a millpond used to store and sort the logs for the sawmill below. The millpond dam measured about 25 feet in height and created a pond approximately 16 feet deep and up to a half-mile long.

This photo taken about 1890 shows "downtown" Loma Prieta. The building on the right is the Loma Prieta Railroad Station. The building on the left is Coates Saloon.
Courtesy: Pajaro Valley Historical Association

Upon reaching the intersection with the Trout Gulch Trail, about 0.5 miles above the sawmill site, you are at the location where the train line crossed over from the west side of Aptos Creek to continue up the canyon. In the open, flat area to your left was the Loma Prieta train station, company store, post office, saloon and boarding house.

Around the next turn is a flat area on the right side of the road where the Loma Prieta schoolhouse once stood. Heading up the fire road you are now back on the old railroad grade as evidenced by railroad ties found in places along the way. Where the road starts to descend toward Aptos Creek, it leaves the railroad grade which continues off to the right.

Just before crossing the footbridge over Aptos Creek, about 0.5 miles beyond the intersection with the Trout Gulch Trail, you will reach the Bottom of the Incline. The incline was a short (2250 feet long) but extremely steep section of narrow-gauge railroad line that went up the side of Aptos Creek Canyon. Completed in 1912, it was used by the Molino Timber Company to transport wood down from their logging operations in the upper regions of today's park. Since the incline was too steep for the train engine, railcars were lowered to the bottom using a steam donkey engine.

After crossing the footbridge over Aptos Creek, you arrive at a sign marking the 1989 Loma Prieta earthquake epicenter area. Here you will find the trailhead for the Aptos Creek Trail. This site was also the location of a 280-foot long curving train trestle that once carried the railroad line up Aptos Creek Canyon.

Beyond the earthquake epicenter area, the road twists up China Ridge through a series of switchbacks. It gains 600 feet in elevation over the next 1.5 miles then reaches a sign announcing the Top of the Incline. Here, the Molino Timber Company lowered narrow-gauge railcars down the incline using a cable controlled by a steam donkey engine. The facilities at this spot included a small switchyard for the train, repair shop and blacksmith shop. About 100 feet below the Top of the Incline, to the left of the road, is a shallow cut in the hillside that marks the steep path of the incline.

After conquering the switchback section you continue to climb, but less steeply since you are now tracing the path of an old narrow-gauge railroad grade for the next 4 miles. The many twists and turns this railroad made prompted Rick Hamman, author of the book

California Central Coast Railways, to call it "one of the crookedest short line narrow-gauge railroads to ever exist in the colorful history of California."

Molino Timber Company's 10-ton wood-burning train engine. It operated for five years above the Top of the Incline.
Courtesy: California Department of Parks & Recreation

About 0.5 miles above the Top of the Incline, you will come to the first of two cement pads on the road. These are oil drilling sites that were installed in the late 1940s. Almost 2 miles further, you will reach an intersection with the trail to Whites Lagoon. One of two small lagoons or ponds in the park, the area around Whites Lagoon was at one time considered a promising location to find oil.

Almost a mile beyond the trail to Whites Lagoon is Sand Point Overlook which, at an elevation of 1600 feet, offers a clear view toward the city of Santa Cruz. The Legend of the Lost Engine has it that a 10-ton train engine is buried under rocks and debris somewhere below this overlook.

Past Sand Point, the fire road turns in a northeasterly direction, still following the railroad grade for the next mile. To your left is Hinckley Creek Canyon, the steepest watershed in the park. It presented the loggers with so many problems that it took three separate logging operations a span of 18 years to denude it of its redwoods.

One mile beyond Sand Point is the location of Camp 2, a small logging camp built about 1914. It was populated by Japanese workers who produced "split stuff" (shingles, posts, pickets, etc.) for the Molino Timber Company. This is where the old railroad grade and fire road part ways. Over the next 1.5 miles, the road continues steeply along the side of China Ridge to an area called Lone Tree Prairie.

Camp 2 with Japanese workers standing in front of possibly one of the first hot tub facilities in Santa Cruz County.
Courtesy: California Department of Parks & Recreation

Lone Tree is marked by a large, fire-scarred, old-growth redwood on the left side of the road. In this area, the lumber company anchored a mile-long overhead cable. The cable was coupled to a steam donkey engine and used to lift split stuff out of Hinckley Basin, an area so steep that not even mules could carry the wood out.

One-half mile above Lone Tree is Sheep Camp Meadow. In the late 1930s, the land in this area was leased to a sheepherder and a cabin built for him at the lower end of the meadow. However, it didn't take long to realize this was no place to raise sheep and the operation was abandoned.

After leaving Sheep Camp Meadow, the road continues to climb moderately for 0.5 miles, then turns in an easterly direction along Santa Rosalia Ridge near the park's northern boundary. As the road levels out at an elevation of 2500 feet, your efforts are rewarded with a sweeping view south toward Watsonville. Across the road from the overlook is a trailhead to the Soquel Demonstration State Forest trail system.

Continuing east, the fire road undulates along Santa Rosalia Ridge for about a mile before coming to the upper locked gate.

Aptos Creek Trail

Trailhead: 1.5 miles north of Porter Family Picnic Area on Aptos Creek Fire Road

Distance: 4.0 miles to intersection with Big Slide Trail
5.0 miles to Five Finger Falls

Elevation Gain: 450 feet

Classification: Easy to moderate over the first 1.5 miles
Strenuous to moderate thereafter

Usage:

HIGHLIGHTS – This trail crosses the Zayante earthquake fault as it winds through flood ravaged Aptos Creek Canyon, rewarding the hiker with a beautiful creekside setting at Five Finger Falls.

Artist's rendering of the 280-foot long curving trestle. The drawing was used by the Southern Pacific Railroad to advertise scenes along their Pajaro and Santa Cruz Railroad.

Courtesy: California State Library, Sacramento, California

This trail begins at the earthquake epicenter area sign 1.5 miles above the the Porter Family Picnic Area. Here in late 1883 or early 1884, the Southern Pacific Railroad Company erected a 280-foot long curving trestle to enter Aptos Creek Canyon. The trail immediately drops down to and crosses Aptos Creek (no bridge), climbs the opposite side then joins the old railbed briefly through a level area before descending for a second creek crossing. About 0.5 miles up the trail, you will arrive at another reminder of the 1989 Loma Prieta earthquake, a sign marker near a jumble of logs at the base of a 150-foot landslide.

Continuing up the canyon, the trail undulates along the ridge while staying close to the murmuring stream. Here, redwood trees share space with big leaf maples, red alders and sycamores with shimmering leaves that make for attractive autumn colors.

About 1 mile from the trailhead you will reach the area where the Loma Prieta Lumber Company built a sawmill and lumber camp in 1884. It was called Monte Vista and for a brief while was the largest mill in Santa Cruz County. This notoriety was short lived however, as Monte Vista burned to the ground in May 1885. A decision was then made to continue the railroad line about two and a half miles further up the canyon. Because of unstable sandy soil and steep canyon

Monte Vista.
Courtesy: California Department of Parks & Recreation

walls, it has been said that this line was "one of the highest priced per mile operations that the Southern Pacific Railroad ever had." Each rainy season hillsides would give way, wiping out whole sections of the railroad.

Over the next 0.5 miles, the trail slowly gains elevation. In places it follows the old railroad grade and crosses an occasional small landslide before reaching Hell's Gate Gulch through which the Zayante earthquake fault travels as it crosses through the park.

After making your way through the massive landslide at Hell's Gate, you will soon leave the creek behind and begin a steep ascent of the nearly vertical canyon wall. Over the next 0.75 miles, the trail snakes up the ridge gaining 250 feet in elevation. After descending through a series of short switchbacks, you will arrive at a small marshy spot called Emerald Pond perched on top of the gulch.

During the next 0.5 miles from Emerald Pond to the intersection with the Big Slide Trail, you will walk through a mixed evergreen forest of redwood, Douglas fir, tan oak and California laurel trees. The trail briefly turns into the forest before returning to the canyon rim which it follows to the lower end of the Big Slide area. Here, during the 1989 Loma Prieta earthquake, debris avalanches denuded over a half-mile of the steep canyon wall. The cracks visible in the ground along the trail in this area were also caused by this earthquake.

Upon reaching the Big Slide Trail, the hardy hiker may choose to loop back to the trailhead by ascending the Big Slide Trail (600-foot elevation gain) to Whites Lagoon and then return down Aptos Creek Fire Road.

From the intersection with the Big Slide Trail, it's another mile to Five Finger Falls. This section of the trail takes the hiker through some of the most attractive scenery in the park. Heading upstream toward the falls, our trail hugs the top of the creek canyon for about 1000 feet before dipping left into the woods along the west slope of the canyon. Because of its elevation and open sunny exposure, the forest here consists of a mixture of oaks, maples, firs and the occasional grove of redwoods. About 0.5 miles from the intersection with the Big Slide Trail, you reach Aptos Creek and enter a thicket of water-loving horsetail ferns. The trail follows the creek through a glen of alders, maples and tan oak trees before entering a shady redwood grove with ground cover of redwood sorrel, sword ferns and five finger ferns. Crossing over a narrow feeder creek on a small footbridge, the trail soon comes to and crosses Aptos Creek. It was in this peaceful creekside setting that the Loma Prieta Lumber Company built their second logging camp in upper Aptos Creek Canyon, Monte Vista

Station. Although nothing remains from that operation, Monte Vista Station enjoyed its glory days in the 1890s. In addition to logging activities, it attracted and accommodated tourists much in the same fashion as the town of Loma Prieta.

Over the next 0.25 miles to Five Finger Falls, the trail climbs gradually and parallels the old railroad line. It then descends back to the creekbed as the canyon walls narrow. Here you will notice a deep, emerald green pool which in summer harbors a population of steelhead trout awaiting the winter rains to head further upstream. At the streambed, walk up the creek canyon and within a few yards you will reach 15-foot high Five Finger Falls which is fed by a perennial stream coming in from the right. You may also notice a number of bent railroad rails laying in and around the creekbed. These are some of the few remaining clues that remind us of the extensive logging operations that once took place in this canyon.

Aptos Rancho Trail

Trailhead: The main trailhead is at the end of Aptos Rancho
Road which intersects with Soquel Drive in Aptos –
This trail is also accessible from other trailheads
along the Aptos Creek Road or at its northern end
near George's Picnic Area

Distances: 0.4 miles to Aptos Creek
0.7 miles to junction with Split Stuff Trail
1.1 miles to junction with Terrace Trail
1.3 miles to junction with Vienna Woods Trail
1.9 miles to trail's end at George's Picnic Area

Elevation Gain: Approximately 100 feet

Classification: Easy to moderate

Usage:

*HIGHLIGHTS – This trail is on property that was once part of the
Aptos Rancho land grant awarded to Rafael Castro by the Mexican
government in 1833. Along this route, you will travel through open,
sunny areas and the cool, shady Aptos Creek Canyon.*

From the trailhead you will descend briefly on a broad, dirt path
which levels out and narrows near a log pile on your right. These logs
were washed downstream during a heavy rainstorm in January 1982
that turned Aptos Creek into a raging torrent. Another log pile is
located about a mile further up this trail.

Beyond the log pile, the trail gradually rises and falls over 0.3 miles
and then arrives at Aptos Creek. After crossing the creek on some
rocks, you will enter a level, sunny area with horsetail ferns growing
in abundance, then return to the shady forest as the trail climbs to
an intersection with the Split Stuff Trail. Your trail now briefly parallels the nearby Aptos Creek Road through a tangle of pampas grass,
scotch broom and blackberry bushes before turning left and descending toward Aptos Creek. As the trail levels out in a dense redwood
grove, you will reach an intersection with the south end of the
Terrace Trail near the second log pile.

The fern-lined path now stays close to Aptos Creek as it winds through a water-loving creekside plant community of redwood trees, big leaf maples, red alders and willows. Soon you will arrive at an intersection with the Vienna Woods Trail which merges briefly with the Aptos Rancho Trail as you climb up a short but steep hill. At the top, the Aptos Rancho Trail turns left at Tillman Memorial Grove while the Vienna Woods Trail continues up to Aptos Creek Road. After leaving the memorial grove, you will climb gradually for a short distance, then turn left at a trail marker. Within a few yards, you will come to the first of a few spur trails that lead down to the creek. The Aptos Rancho Trail continues to the right, winding along the canyon wall, then descends to the creek where it intersects again with the Terrace Trail. Turning right, your trail climbs moderately, crossing a couple of seasonal creeks before arriving at the canyon rim. *(Don't be alarmed if you hear loud animal noises in this area. Some peacocks live on private property across the canyon and sometimes make quite a ruckus.)* From the canyon rim the trail quickly crosses through the forest to George's Picnic Area.

Big Slide Trail

Trailhead: Near Whites Lagoon

Distance: 1.5 miles

Elevation Loss: 600 feet

Classification: Moderate to strenuous

Usage:

HIGHLIGHTS – A convenient shortcut from Whites Lagoon to upper Aptos Creek Canyon and the scenic Five Finger Falls area. This trail also descends one the steepest ridges in the park dropping 600 feet over a distance of about 1 mile.

The Big Slide Trail begins at a marked sign post on the Whites Lagoon Trail 0.2 miles from the Aptos Creek Fire Road. After leaving the trailhead you will descend, gradually at first, under a shady forest canopy of oaks and Douglas firs. The trail soon comes to the face of the ridge high above Aptos Creek before descending steeply over the next mile through a series of switchbacks. Because of the steep terrain and unstable soil, this area is prone to landslides during heavy winter rains. As a result of the ground movement, many trees grow at odd angles along this section of the trail.

Soon after reaching the bottom of the switchback section, the Big Slide Trail intersects the Aptos Creek Trail at the canyon rim overlooking Aptos Creek which is about 150 feet below. This portion of Aptos Creek Canyon was denuded by landslides caused by the Loma Prieta earthquake of 1989. A right turn at this trail intersection will lead you downstream to the Aptos Creek Fire Road, a distance of about 4 miles. A left turn will take you 1 mile upstream to Five Finger Falls.

Bridge Creek Trail

Trailhead: Bridge Creek Trailhead sign
(0.9 miles up the Loma Prieta Grade Trail)

Distance: 1.4 miles one way

Elevation Gain: 150 feet to Bridge Creek Historic Site

Classification: Moderate

Usage: 🚶

HIGHLIGHTS – This trail follows sections of the old 30 inch narrow-gauge railroad line (built in 1917) up the creek canyon to the Bridge Creek Historic Site.

The trail to Bridge Creek Historic Site begins at a trail sign about a mile up the Loma Prieta Grade Trail. At the trail signpost, the Loma Prieta Grade Trail turns left and leads up to Hoffman's Historic Site while the Bridge Creek Trail heads straight on a level path through an oak forest. As you walk along, notice the railroad ties still in place. The trail soon leads to the edge of Bridge Creek Canyon, then winds along the canyon wall before coming to a seasonal creek which has formed a grotto of waterworn boulders. Looking across the creek canyon you will notice landslides, the result of winter storm erosion and earthquake activity.

Shortly before the halfway point, the trail drops down to Bridge Creek. Before you cross the creek, look up to your left. The massive logs stacked on top of each other once supported the train line which continued along this side of the canyon for another 0.3 miles then crossed over to the east side of the creek on a trestle.

Over the next half-mile to the Bridge Creek Historic Site, the trail undulates through the canyon and climbs steeply (but briefly) in places. Shortly before reaching the historic site, you will come upon impressive evidence of the effort to extend the railroad up this canyon. In a shady grove of redwoods are the remains of a bridge of horizontal logs held up by a stack of large redwood support logs. This functioned as an inexpensive trestle that was strong enough to bear the weight of a 14-ton train engine.

Continuing upstream, the trail soon drops down to the Bridge Creek Historic Site. This was the location of a small logging camp built by the Loma Prieta Lumber Company in 1917. The Bridge Creek camp consisted of several small shanties built on both sides of the creek. Most of the cabins were washed away during a violent rainstorm in January 1982, but the ruins of two shacks are still noticeable at the site.

The railroad line probably extended up the canyon to Maple Falls but extensive storm damage has wiped out all evidence. To reach 30-foot high Maple Falls, continue up Bridge Creek Canyon about 0.5 miles on an indistinct trail that is best taken during dry months.

One of the cabins at Bridge Creek Historic Site.

Courtesy: Ron Powell

To return, you can either backtrack on the Bridge Creek Trail or continue on a loop trail through Hoffman's Historic Site. To complete the loop through the historic sites, cross Bridge Creek at the historic site then climb steeply 0.6 miles up Big Tree Gulch. From the top of Big Tree Gulch to Hoffman's Historic Site, it is another 0.8 miles on a level grade.

Buggy Trail

Trailhead: George's Picnic Area
Distance: 0.5 miles one way
Elevation Gain: Approximately 100 feet
Classification: Easy
Usage:

HIGHLIGHTS – A leisurely stroll on this easy trail will complement a lazy day at George's Picnic Area.

Bordered by sword ferns, this short trail heads south from George's Picnic Area on a level grade before gently climbing into an oak forest. After a brief descent, you arrive at Aptos Creek Road.

You have three trails to choose from for your return to the picnic area: 1) retrace your steps on the Buggy Trail; 2) turn right and follow the Aptos Creek Road; or 3) cross over the road and connect with the Aptos Rancho Trail.

To return via Aptos Rancho Trail, cross the road and take the Vienna Woods Trail going downhill. Within about 200 feet, you will connect with the Aptos Rancho Trail at Tillman Memorial Grove. Turn right and follow the trail as it winds along the hillside between the road and Aptos Creek through a shady forest of second-growth redwood trees. It will end across from the George's Picnic Area parking lot.

Hinckley Fire Road

Trailhead: Sand Point Overlook

Distances: 0.4 miles to West Ridge Trail Camp
3.0 miles to the park boundary
3.5 miles to Olive Springs Road

Elevation Loss: 150 feet to trail camp
1,600 feet to Hinckley Creek

Classification: Strenuous

Usage:

HIGHLIGHTS – The Hinckley Creek watershed is one of the most steep and difficult areas to hike in Santa Cruz County. From its head-waters at an elevation of 2600 feet along Santa Rosalia Ridge, the creek drops 2200 feet in only four and a half miles. Its twisting course and nearly vertical canyon walls presented the loggers with so many problems that it took three separate logging operations 18 years to strip Hinckley Basin of its redwoods.

Loggers working on a tree in Hinckley Basin.
Courtesy: California Department of Parks & Recreation

The Hinckley Fire Road was built in 1936 and follows the route of a skid road constructed about 1900 by the Loma Prieta Lumber Company. It was used to haul logs down to their sawmill on Hinckley Creek.

From its intersection with Aptos Creek Fire Road at Sand Point Overlook, the Hinckley Fire Road winds down the ridge 0.4 miles to the West Ridge Trail Camp. The land on your left through this section is called the "split stuff area," a half-mile wide portion of upper Bridge Creek Canyon. From 1912-1918, split stuff (grape stakes, pickets, posts etc.) was produced here then loaded on the Molino Timber Company train at Sand Point.

Legend has it that a 10-ton train engine, named the "Betsy Jane," was hauled into the split stuff area to move logs and split wood. Then in September 1918, a heavy rainstorm caused the railroad line to slip away, sending the engine 100 feet down the hill. Today, the Betsy Jane may be resting somewhere within the split stuff area buried under tons of rocks and debris.

From the trail camp, the fire road descends very steeply over the next mile to a locked gate. Shortly beyond the gate, the road levels out near an intersection with another portion of the fire road leading off to the left. Bear right at this intersection. As you walk along this level section, you might catch a glimpse of a small sunken meadow on the left. This meadow was once a small lake dug for a 61-site housing development planned by millionaire, Allen Rispin, of Capitola. He was busy making improvements to the property when the stock market crash of 1929 wiped out his financial empire. The property changed owners and cabins were built during the 1930s. When the Hinckley Creek watershed became part of the state park in 1965, a number of the housing sites were still privately owned and several homes had been built. Over the years, most of the original owners have sold their land to the state and now there are only a few houses still in private ownership. Beyond the old lake bed, you will soon come to another intersection in the road that leads left to the few privately owned houses. Please respect their privacy and do not enter this area.

Proceeding past the housing development, the Hinckley Fire Road winds down the canyon through a series of turns. In about 0.5 miles, you will reach a flat area on the right across the road from a private house. Here in 1907, the Loma Prieta Lumber Company built a sawmill but dismantled it before the first log was cut. To understand the reason why, we need to go back to the year 1901.

Thirsting after the millions of board feet of lumber in Hinckley Creek Canyon, the Loma Prieta Lumber Company built a sawmill along lower Hinckley Creek. Their operations progressed well over the next few years until the night of January 18, 1906, when a heavy thunderstorm hit the area. The resulting water runoff rushed down the canyon causing the millpond dam to break. The logs in the millpond, now floating loose, turned into battering rams, destroying the downstream mill. It was decided to rebuild the sawmill and work began immediately. Three months later, in the early morning of April 18, 1906, the construction crew rebuilding the mill had just risen to another work day when at 5:15 am, disaster struck again in the form of the great earthquake of 1906. A mass of earth estimated at 100 feet in depth, filled the canyon burying the men living in the nearby cabins. Nine men died that morning. Despite the efforts of 150 laborers, it took weeks to recover the bodies.

The story now returns to the flat area next to the fire road. Rather than attempting to rebuild the mill down in the creek canyon, the lumber company selected a site at the flat area about 350 feet higher up on the ridge. By early 1907, the new mill's machinery was ready to be installed when a decision was suddenly made to dismantle it and pursue other plans. That decision was probably based on a number of factors, not the least of which was the difficulty and expense the company would face moving logs to their new mill. Mother Nature won this round but the loggers would be back six years later for another try.

Heading down the fire road, you will reach the park boundary in about 0.5 miles and then Hinckley Creek in another 50 yards. Beyond the park boundary, the road continues on a right-of-way through private property for another half-mile and requires 4 unbridged creek crossings before reaching Olive Springs Road. This may be difficult or dangerous especially during or after periods of rain.

Loma Prieta Grade Trail

Trailhead: 0.2 miles north of Porter Family Picnic Area on Aptos Creek Fire Road

Distances: 0.7 miles to Porter House Site
0.9 miles to Bridge Creek Trailhead
2.3 miles to Hoffman's Historic Site
2.3 miles to Bridge Creek Historic Site via Bridge Creek Trail
6.0 miles to complete historic loop

Elevation Gain: 50 feet to Bridge Creek Trailhead
350 feet to Hoffman's Historic Site

Classification: Easy to moderate

Usage: 🚶

HIGHLIGHTS – The first section of this popular trail leads to the Porter House Site by tracing the railroad grade built in 1883. The Loma Prieta Grade Trail continues past the connection with the Bridge Creek Trail and up to Hoffman's Historic Site, the best preserved logging camp in the park.

After walking 0.2 miles up the Aptos Creek Fire Road from the Porter Family Picnic Area parking lot, you will notice a trail sign on your left announcing the Loma Prieta Grade Trail. The trail begins on a slight upward incline shaded by redwoods, tan oaks and maple trees as it follows the old railroad grade. Soon you will come to a small creek over which the trains once rumbled on a 95-foot long wooden trestle. Here your trail leaves the railroad bed, drops down to the creek and crosses a wooden footbridge. Just beyond the footbridge, the trail climbs briefly then turns to the left. As it levels out, look to your right and you will see the old train trestle timbers laying in a pile with bracken ferns growing among them.

You are now back on the railroad bed going north, parallel with Aptos Creek on your right. This section of the trail offers "clues" to the logging era in the form of rusty metal cables and the occasional railroad tie. Along the right side of the trail, look for the rotting remnants of a wooden ramp over which logs tumbled down into the millpond below. It was also in this area in 1919 that a train wreck was staged for a movie titled "One Way Trail."

As the forest canopy gives way to an open area, you are approaching the Porter House Site, which is marked by a sign. Warren Porter was the secretary for the Loma Prieta Lumber Company and lived in a comfortable house on this site with his wife Mary Easton and son John. Warren Porter later became Lieutenant Governor of the State of California in 1907. In addition to the Porter family house, there was a cottage for the lumber company's board of directors, who held their monthly meetings at this location. The directors cottage consisted of a dining room, kitchen and quarters for the cook plus bedrooms for the seven directors. Today, there is nothing left of these buildings except their foundations and a few loose bricks. Across from the Porter House Site the main railroad line crossed over Aptos Creek on a 210-foot long, 60-foot high bridge. At the other end of this bridge was the Loma Prieta Railroad Station, company store, post office, saloon and boarding house.

Also across from the Porter House Site is the Mill Pond Trail. It will lead you over Aptos Creek on a footbridge then up to the fire road. From there, you can loop back to the parking area by following the road.

Beyond the Porter House Site, the trail stays on a level grade above Aptos Creek and turns left into a seasonal creek canyon over which the lumber trains crossed on another wooden trestle. Look for the bridge timbers and beams in the creekbed as your trail winds into the canyon. After crossing the footbridge and rounding the next corner, you will come to a signed intersection with the Bridge Creek Trail. The Loma Prieta Grade Trail continues left up to Hoffman's Historic Site while the Bridge Creek Trail leads into Bridge Creek Canyon, reaching the Bridge Creek Historic Site in 1.4 miles.

From this intersection it is possible to do a 4.2-mile long loop through Hoffman's and Bridge Creek historic sites. The easier way is to take the Loma Prieta Grade Trail 1.4 miles up to Hoffman's Historic Site then continue 0.8 miles to Big Tree Gulch. A steep trail down Big Tree Gulch leads to the Bridge Creek Historic Site in 0.6 miles. From there it's another 1.4-mile hike down the Bridge Creek Trail to complete the loop.

Loma Prieta Grade Trail to Hoffman's Historic Site

Distance: 1.4 miles from intersection with Bridge Creek Trail
Elevation Gain: 350 feet to historic site
Classification: Moderate

HIGHLIGHTS – This trail leads to the logging camp remains at Hoffman's Historic Site. From there, it is possible to loop back through the Bridge Creek Historic Site or connect with the West Ridge Trail.

After 35 years of logging in the hills above Aptos, the last remaining stand of uncut redwoods for miles around grew on the west slope of Bridge Creek Canyon. Beginning in 1917, the Loma Prieta Lumber Company built a 30 inch narrow-gauge railroad up the lower canyon along Bridge Creek and established a small logging camp they called Camp 4, now known as the Bridge Creek Historic Site. To get logs from the upper slope down to the sawmill at Loma Prieta, the lumber company built another narrow-gauge railroad up the hillside and constructed a second logging camp. Originally called Camp 5, today it is known as Hoffman's Historic Site. This section of the Loma Prieta Grade Trail follows, for the most part, the railroad grade to Hoffman's Historic Site.

From its intersection with the Bridge Creek Trail, the Loma Prieta Grade Trail climbs moderately for 0.2 miles through an oak covered hillside. The logging train maneuvered up and down this hill using a switchback. As the trail levels out, it joins the railroad grade which is marked in many places by old railroad ties. Over the next 0.5 miles, the trail meanders in and out of a few seasonal creek ravines while slowly gaining elevation.

As you approach the fourth seasonal creek, the trail drops down to the creekbed then up the opposite side. The train crossed this gap on a short trestle and a few of the support beams can be seen in the ravine. As the trail crosses over the next ridge, look for a pile of boards about 25 feet to the right of the path. This was once a cabin used by a gardener who grew vegetables which were loaded on the train as it passed on its way up to the logging camp or down to the sawmill cookhouse. The garden was to the left of the trail across from the cabin.

The trail winds through yet another ravine then passes through a narrow gap in the ridge cut for the train line. As you come around the bend the hillside on the right drops off very steeply as the trail hugs the canyon wall for the next 0.3 miles. It was in this vicinity that

Sunday outing to Camp 5 (Hoffman's Historic Site) in background.
Courtesy: Santa Cruz County Historical Trust; Paul Johnston collection

the photo (above) was taken of the two women with the logging camp in the background. The deep canyon narrows as the trail crosses over two footbridges and approaches the historic site. You will begin to see dilapidated cabins on your right and within the next several yards come to a sign marking Hoffman's Historic Site.

Hoffman's Historic Site, about 1920.
Courtesy: Santa Cruz County Historical Trust; Paul Johnston collection

This logging camp was used from 1918-1921 and is named after the camp's superintendent, Louis Hoffman and his wife who was the head cook. Nicknamed "Camp Comfort" by the Hoffmans, it consisted of about 25 buildings including a cookhouse with living quarters for the Hoffmans, a meeting hall, blacksmith shop and corrals and barns for the mules. It also had a 120-foot long bunkhouse with adjoining showers and washrooms plus several cabins used by men who did not want to live in the bunkhouse. This camp is the best "preserved" historic site in the park with the remains of several cabins scattered throughout the general area. Many of these structures remained standing until the late 1960s.

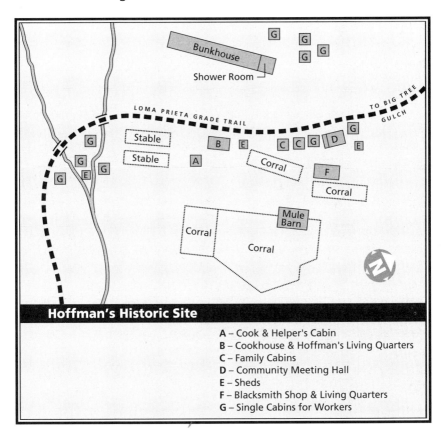

Hoffman's Historic Site

A – Cook & Helper's Cabin
B – Cookhouse & Hoffman's Living Quarters
C – Family Cabins
D – Community Meeting Hall
E – Sheds
F – Blacksmith Shop & Living Quarters
G – Single Cabins for Workers

From the sign marking the historic site, the Big Stump Gap Trail leads up to the West Ridge Trail. It goes through the upper portion of the historic site and climbs moderately for 0.5 miles before intersecting with the Ridge Connection Trail. The Big Stump Gap Trail forks to the right and connects with the West Ridge Trail which goes on to the West Ridge Trail Camp. The Ridge Connection Trail forks to the left at the intersection and also connects with the West Ridge Trail. Upon reaching the West Ridge Trail, a turn to the left takes you back down to Aptos Creek Fire Road. A turn to the right leads to the trail camp.

Hoffman's Historic Site to Bridge Creek Historic Site

Distance: 1.4 miles

Elevation Loss: 240 feet to Bridge Creek Historic Site

Classification: Easy to strenuous (downhill)

HIGHLIGHTS – This trail section continues the historic loop along the old train line to its end at Big Tree Gulch, then down the gulch to Bridge Creek Historic Site.

The Loma Prieta Grade Trail continues through Hoffman's Historic Site along a level grade that follows the railroad line for another 0.8 miles to Big Tree Gulch. This gulch once held some of the largest old-growth redwood trees in Santa Cruz County. As the trail begins to wind down the gulch, you will notice the charred remains of one of those giants. Frederick A. Hihn, a prominent Santa Cruz citizen and lumber company owner, wanted to give these trees and some surrounding land to Santa Cruz County for use as a park. Unfortunately, after his death in 1913, those plans went awry and these great trees succumbed to the ax and saw.

The trail down Big Tree Gulch winds steeply for 0.6 miles to Bridge Creek and the historic site on the opposite bank. To complete the historic loop, turn right at the Bridge Creek Historic Site and continue 1.4 miles on the Bridge Creek Trail to its intersection with the Loma Prieta Grade Trail. *(See Bridge Creek Trail description for details of the trail and Bridge Creek Historic Site.)*

Mill Pond Trail

Trailhead: 0.8 miles beyond the Porter Family Picnic Area
                      on Aptos Creek Fire Road

Distance: 0.1 miles

Classification: Moderate

Usage:

HIGHLIGHTS – This short trail connects the fire road with the Loma Prieta Grade Trail. It crosses Aptos Creek on a bridge through an area once occupied by the Loma Prieta millpond.

Starting on the Aptos Creek Fire Road, the Mill Pond Trail winds down to an attractive spot on Aptos Creek. From the mid 1880s to the early 1920s, this area was the upper end of a millpond used to store and sort logs for the sawmill below. After crossing the creek on a footbridge the trail climbs briefly to the Porter House Site on the Loma Prieta Grade Trail.

Porter Trail

Trailhead: Mary Easton Picnic Area

Distance: 1 mile

Elevation Gain: 200 feet

Classification: Moderate

Usage:

HIGHLIGHTS – This short trail traverses the hillside between the Mary Easton and Porter Family picnic areas.

The Porter Trail hike can start at either the Mary Easton or the Porter Family picnic areas. However, it is an easier walk starting at the Mary Easton Picnic Area. Beginning at the trail sign across the road from the Mary Easton Picnic Area, you quickly descend to Aptos Creek, crossing it on a path of rocks. After reaching the other side, the trail follows the creek upstream for about 50 yards, then turns into a mixed evergreen forest of oak, Douglas fir and redwood trees. The trail begins a gradual climb up the hillside, then becomes steeper as it follows near the path of a seasonal creek. After walking about 0.7 miles, you will reach the top of a ridge and then start a winding descent through the forest, arriving at Aptos Creek across from the Porter Family Picnic Area. Once again, you will cross the creek on some rocks to the picnic area which is located in an attractive spot near a bend on the creek.

You can return the way you came or loop back to the Mary Easton Picnic Area on the Aptos Creek Road.

Split Stuff Trail

Trailhead: The parking lot at the entrance station on Aptos Creek Road

Distance: 0.2 miles to the Aptos Rancho Trail

Classification: Easy

Usage:

HIGHLIGHTS – The Split Stuff Trail provides a connection from the entrance station parking lot to the Aptos Rancho Trail. "Split stuff" refers to wood shingles, posts, pickets and grape stakes that were frequently produced in the woods by hand at the site where the tree had fallen. Many stacks of split stuff were left behind and can still be found by the inquisitive hiker in some remote areas of the park.

This hike starts to the left of the parking lot restroom and within a few yards comes to the main trail. Turn right and walk about 1000 feet through an open, sunny area to the connection with the Aptos Rancho Trail.

A left turn on the Aptos Rancho Trail leads south to Aptos Creek in about 0.3 miles then continues on to its trailhead on Aptos Rancho Road. A right turn at the trail connection leads north through Aptos Creek Canyon to George's Picnic Area.

Terrace Trail

Trailhead: 0.6 miles beyond the entrance station on Aptos Rancho Trail

Distances: 0.6 miles to junction with Vienna Woods Trail
1.0 miles to George's Picnic Area

Elevation Loss: Approximately 100 feet

Classification: Easy to moderate

Usage: 

HIGHLIGHTS – The Terrace Trail takes the visitor through many scenic areas along Aptos Creek.

To reach the Terrace Trail from the entrance station parking lot, take the Split Stuff Trail 0.2 miles to the Aptos Rancho Trail, then turn right and continue 0.4 miles to the trailhead sign located near a stack of redwood logs. These logs were washed downstream during a heavy rainstorm in January 1982 that turned Aptos Creek into a turbulent stream of mud, logs and debris.

From the trailhead, your path immediately descends to and crosses Aptos Creek (no bridge) and then enters a thicket of alder trees growing along the creek. The trail soon begins a moderate climb as it twists through a redwood grove before leveling out. Continuing on a level grade for about 0.3 miles through a mixed evergreen forest, the trail soon passes through an area that from spring through fall is covered with lacy bracken ferns and sword ferns. After crossing a small footbridge, you quickly arrive at an intersection with the Vienna Woods Trail.

The Terrace Trail crosses the Vienna Woods Trail and heads down toward Aptos Creek, dipping into a seasonal creekbed shortly before crossing another small creek on a short footbridge. The trail now undulates through the redwoods and arrives at Aptos Creek. Keep an eye out here for kingfisher birds, which fly along the creek corridor searching for food.

After rock-hopping across the creek, turn left and follow the trail upstream for about 200 feet to its end at the intersection with Aptos Rancho Trail.

To reach George's Picnic Area, continue straight ahead on what is now the Aptos Rancho Trail as it winds up to the rim of Aptos Creek Canyon. This path quickly crosses through the forest to the picnic area.

Trout Gulch Trail

Trailhead: On Aptos Creek Fire Road 1 mile north of the Porter Family Picnic Area

Distance: 2 miles round trip

Elevation Gain: 450 feet

Classification: Moderate

Usage:

HIGHLIGHTS – This trail leads up to the ridgetop that forms the southeast boundary of the park.

The open area opposite the trailhead was once the commercial and business center of the town of Loma Prieta. Located along both sides of the railroad tracks were the railroad station, company store, post office, saloon and boarding house.

The lower section of the Trout Gulch Trail briefly parallels an old railroad spur line before climbing up the canyon, carved by a seasonal creek. The warm, south-facing side of the canyon offers a perfect habitat for a mixture of oak and fragrant bay trees. In the autumn months, leaves falling from these trees cover the trail in a colorful carpet of orange, gold and red.

About 0.5 miles from the trailhead, the steep canyon relaxes and forms a broader floor. Here you will see clumps of redwood trees, which prefer the cooler north-facing slopes. The trail levels out as it crosses through a small forest meadow before making one last ascent to the top of the ridge.

At the ridgetop, the trail veers left and offers an occasional glimpse of Aptos Creek Canyon on your left. Continuing along the ridge, the trail drops slightly then makes a right turn in an oak forest as it approaches the park boundary which is marked by a wooden fence and post. The official park boundary sign has vanished, so use the wooden fence as your turnaround point. Proceeding any further leads to private property. A pleasant downhill return trip is your reward as you retrace your steps to the fire road.

Vienna Woods Trail

Trailhead: On Aptos Creek Road across from the south end of the Buggy Trail

Distances: 200 feet to Tillman Memorial Grove
0.1 miles to Aptos Creek
0.4 miles to junction with Terrace Trail
0.9 miles to Mesa Grande Road

Elevation Gain: Approximately 200 feet to trail's end

Classification: Easy to moderate

Usage:

HIGHLIGHTS – While relatively short, the Vienna Woods Trail travels through two of the three vegetation zones in the park: creekside riparian and mixed evergreen.

From its start on Aptos Creek Road, the Vienna Woods Trail begins on a downslope reaching the Tillman Memorial Grove within 200 feet. There it merges briefly with the Aptos Rancho Trail on a broad path down a steep hill. At the bottom, the Vienna Woods Trail branches right, down to and across Aptos Creek.

Once across the creek, the trail turns north staying close to the creek as it winds through a lush riparian (creekside) plant community that is populated by redwood, big leaf maple and alder trees. Sword and bracken ferns line the trail. The trail then begins to climb slightly arriving at a place where, from the left, two unmarked paths come down from the Terrace Trail. Proceeding straight ahead, the trail descends to a low area that stays wet most of the year. Here you will find a variety of water-loving plants including ginger, forget-me-not, wild rose and redwood violet. Your trail soon comes to a fork where a right turn quickly leads to a pleasant redwood grove next to the creek. The Vienna Woods Trail bears left at this fork and goes uphill to a plateau and an intersection with the Terrace Trail. Your route continues through the trail intersection for about 50 yards then turns left and climbs on a moderate grade over the next-half mile to the park boundary.

Leaving the creekside plant community, the trail climbs up a shady canyon into a mixed evergreen forest of redwood and Douglas fir trees. After making a hairpin turn, the trail winds out of the canyon to a warm, exposed ridge where oak and madrone trees grow along with sun-tolerant bracken ferns.

After crossing over the ridge, the trail climbs along the edge of another shady canyon that is home to many redwood trees. In contrast, on the right side of the trail, the redwoods give way to oak and manzanita trees that grow along the exposed ridge. Ground cover along this section of the trail consists of yerba buena, hairy honeysuckle, coffee berry, forget-me-not and the ever-present poison oak. Soon you will reach the trail's end at a private dirt road near the Vienna Woods subdivision.

West Ridge Trail

Trailhead: 0.5 miles beyond George's Picnic Area on
Aptos Creek Road

Distances: 2.0 miles to power lines
5.0 miles to overview area
6.0 miles to West Ridge Trail Camp

Elevation Gain: 650 feet to power lines
1000 feet to Ridge Connection Trail
1100 feet to overview area
1200 feet to West Ridge Trail Camp

Classification: Moderate to strenuous

Usage:

HIGHLIGHTS – As the name implies, this trail climbs a mountain ridge which it follows to the West Ridge Trail Camp. The hiker is rewarded with good views along the way.

The trail begins on an easy uphill grade that briefly traces the path of an old railroad spur line up the shady creek canyon. (Keep an eye out for an old piece of rail bordering the trail on your left.) After crossing the creek on a wooden footbridge, the trail climbs moderately up and along the side of the canyon. The redwood trees you see growing in this area are a good example of the "family circle" of young redwoods that grow around the base of a tree that has been cut. Growing from the roots of the "mother tree," they have an advantage over trees that grow from seeds, since from the start they have the root system of the parent to feed them. Up to 50 new trees may form the circle, but as they compete for light, most will die until only one or two of the strongest and most rapidly growing trees remain.

About 0.5 miles up the canyon, the trail crosses the creek at a hairpin turn. You now leave the cool canyon environment behind as the trail winds moderately up and across a hillside through a grove of tan oak trees mixed with Douglas firs. After climbing for almost a mile, the trail reaches a ridge and becomes less steep.

Around the 2-mile point, you will come to a junction with a dirt road. Turn right and shortly you will reach PG&E power lines which run in a northwesterly direction. To your right is Aptos Creek Canyon. To your left is the Bates Creek watershed which forms the park's western boundary in this area. Shortly after 1900, 115 acres above Bates Creek were slated for development as a housing project to be named Arden Forest from the Shakespeare play "As You Like It." The developers went as far as building the roads and laying out 62 homesites but the project was never completed. Currently, there are no trails leading into this section of the park.

Shortly after passing the power lines, your trail branches to the left leaving the road at a large Douglas fir tree. It continues on a winding path just below the ridgetop for about 0.7 miles, then finally reaches the top of the ridge near the 3-mile point. From here, the trail undulates along the ridge while gaining 200 feet in elevation as it approaches a junction with the Ridge Connection Trail.

The Ridge Connection Trail will lead you a mile down to Hoffman's Historic Site. From there, it is possible to loop back to the West Ridge Trailhead by hiking down the Loma Prieta Grade Trail which in turn connects with the Aptos Creek Fire Road.

Over the next 0.5 miles the trail briefly skirts the western boundary of the park, then comes to an intersection with the Big Stump Gap Trail, which also connects to Hoffman's Historic Site.

The next section of trail to the West Ridge Trail Camp covers a distance of about 1.5 miles over moderate to steep terrain. Your route parallels an old trail on the ridge above that existed prior to 1860. If you are brave enough to tromp up the hillside through the poison oak, you may find several large redwood logs and piles of split wood laying around, evidence of early logging activity.

About 0.5 miles beyond the Big Stump Gap Trail, you will come to an opening in the trees along a small landslide. The view is southeast across upper Bridge Creek Canyon and beyond to the Aptos Creek watershed. A sign nearby indicates a quarter-mile spur trail down to Thompson's Bench where you can sit and enjoy the view. Thompson's Bench is named after Don Thompson, the Marks' family real estate broker. He also acted as their middle man during negotiations with the State of California and the Nature Conservancy to deed the Marks' land holdings and create the state park you now enjoy.

The final mile to the trail camp climbs up to and along a narrow ridgetop through a mixed evergreen forest. It then descends to the trail camp located on the Hinckley Fire Road. If you have the energy, turn right and walk 0.4 miles up to Sand Point Overlook. From there you can walk down the Aptos Creek Fire Road about 6.5 miles to the West Ridge Trailhead to complete a 13-mile loop.

Whites Lagoon Trail

Trailhead: 5.2 miles north of Porter Family Picnic Area on Aptos Creek Fire Road

Distance: 0.4 miles

Elevation Gain: 60 feet

Classification: Easy to moderate

Usage:

HIGHLIGHTS – This short trail leads to one of two ponds within the park and to the Big Slide Trailhead.

Spur trails and old roads lead from the broad trail as it winds through a mixed forest of redwoods, bay trees and tan oaks. In about 0.2 miles, you come to the trail signpost noting that Whites Lagoon is 0.2 miles straight ahead. At the signpost, the Big Slide Trail bears right and reaches the Aptos Creek Trail in about 1.5 miles.

Perched on a steep slope high above Aptos Creek Canyon, Whites Lagoon is fed by winter rain and holds water year-round. While its water level varies with the amount of rainfall, it is usually very shallow and partially covered with reeds, grass and willows. Extensive feral pig activity is evident in the disturbed soil and mudbath holes around the shore.

INDEX

Amphibians, 20
Aptos Creek, 1, 6, 16, 17, 20, 21, 37, 38, 40, 42, 55
Aptos Creek Road/Fire Road, 3, 4, 6, 23, 30-35, 36
Aptos Creek Trail, 29, 33, 36-39, 42,
Aptos Rancho Trail, 29, 40-41
Banana Slug, 21
Bates Creek, 64
Bicycle Regulations, 6
Big Slide Trail, 29, 42
Big Stump Gap Trail, 29, 54, 64
Big Tree Gulch, 44, 50, 54
Birds, 21, 41, 58
Bottom of the Incline, 13, 33
Bridge Creek, 1, 13, 16, 43, 44, 51, 54
Bridge Creek Historic Site, 13, 29, 43, 44, 49, 50
Bridge Creek Trail, 29, 43-44
Buggy Trail, 6, 29, 45
Buzzard Lagoon, 14
Camp 2, 15, 34, 35
Campground, 4, see also West Ridge Trail Camp
Castro, Martina, 7
Castro, Rafael, 40
China Ridge, 16, 33, 34
Earthquake, 1989 Loma Prieta, 1, 13, 16-19, 38, 42
Earthquake, 1906, 17, 48
Easton, Mary, 5, 12, 50
Emerald Pond, 38
Equestrian Regulations, 6
Five Finger Falls, 29, 36, 38, 39 42
George's Picnic Area, 4, 11, 27, 29, 45
Hell's Gate, 18, 38
Hihn, Frederick, 54
Hinckley Creek, 1, 16, 17, 46-48
Hinckley Fire Road, 29, 46-48, 65
Hoffman, Louis, 12, 53
Hoffman's Historic Site, 12-13, 29, 43, 44, 49, 50-54, 64
Loma Prieta Town, 8, 9, 11, 12, 25, 32, 60
Loma Prieta Grade Trail, 29,31, 49-54
Loma Prieta Lumber Company, 5, 7, 25, 37, 38, 44, 47, 48, 50, 51
Loma Prieta Mill Site, 11, 27, 29, 30, 32, 33, 37
Lone Tree Prairie, 15, 34, 35

Mammals, 20, 66
Maple Falls, 13, 44
Marks, Nisene, 2, 10
Mary Easton Picnic Area, 5, 29, 30, 56
Mill Pond Trail, 29, 50, 55
Molino Timber Company, 13, 14, 15, 33, 34, 47
Monte Vista, 37
Monte Vista Station, 38, 39
Native Americans, 25
Nature Conservancy, 2, 10, 64
Porter Family Picnic Area, 5, 6, 27, 29, 56
Porter House Site, 12, 25, 27, 29, 49, 50
Porter Trail, 29, 56
Porter, Warren, 5, 12, 50
Rancho Soquel Augmentation, 7
Regulations, 6
Reptiles, 20, 21
Ridge Connection Trail, 29, 54, 63, 64
Rispin, Allen, 47
San Andreas Fault, 1, 18, 19
Sand Point Overlook, 15, 29, 34, 46, 47
Santa Rosalia Ridge, 1, 3, 35, 46
Save-The-Redwood League, 10
Sheep Camp Meadow, 35
Soquel Creek, 1, 18
Soquel Demonstration State Forest, 3, 29, 30, 35
Southern Pacific Railroad Company, 8, 37
Split Stuff, 9, 13, 34, 35, 47, 57
Split Stuff Trail, 29, 57
Steam Donkey, 14, 15, 33, 35
Terrace Trail, 29, 58-59
Thompson's Bench, 64
Tillman Grove, 41, 45, 61
Top of the Incline, 14, 30, 33, 34
Trail Distances, 29
Trails, selecting, 27-28
Trees & Plants, 22-26
Trout Gulch Trail, 29, 33, 60
Van Eck Tree, 23, 31
Vienna Woods Trail, 29, 41, 61-62
Weather, 4
West Ridge Trail, 4, 29, 54, 63-65
West Ridge Trail Camp, 4, 6, 29, 47, 54, 63, 64
Whites Lagoon, 14, 17, 29, 34, 42, 66
Whites Lagoon Trail, 29, 66
Wildlife, 20-21
Zayante Fault, 1, 18, 19, 36, 38

How You Can Help the Park...

Join the Advocates For Nisene Marks State Park

The Advocates For Nisene Marks State Park is a nonprofit corporation founded by local community members to support the park. With over 140 members, the Advocates is a strong partner for the California Department of Parks in helping provide capital improvements and implementing special projects. As the state budget cutbacks have severely hampered the ability of the Department of Parks to upgrade and maintain the park, it is necessary for the active park user to pitch in and help. Through the Advocates, park users, with donations of time and/or money, can help maintain trails, build capital improvement projects (such as building an outhouse or decking a new bridge), sponsor special events (such as a slide show on the history of the park), and work to address the sometimes conflicting needs of the various user groups.

Your tax deductible donation and volunteer time will help:

- Fund capital improvements
- Assist in park maintenance
- Improve and maintain trails
- Sponsor projects in the park
- Work to balance interests of various user groups
- Communicate park user needs to state park management

Please make your check payable to "Advocates"

Send to:

The Advocates For
Nisene Marks State Park
Post Office Box 461
Aptos, CA 95001-0461

Join us today!

Advocates For Nisene Marks State Park
MEMBERSHIP APPLICATION

NAME _____

ADDRESS _____

CITY _____ STATE _____ ZIP _____

PHONE _____ FAX _____

SPECIAL INTEREST _____

_____

Annual Membership:

❑ Family $30   ❑ Sponsor $150
❑ Individual $20   ❑ Patron $250
❑ Student $10   ❑ Benefactor $500
❑ Associate $75

You will be notified by mail of the date of our next meeting.

NOTES

NOTES

Order Form

Please send me _____ copies of **Explore...** *The Forest of Nisene Marks State Park* @ $9.95 per copy.

DATE
_____

NAME
_____

MAILING ADDRESS
_____

CITY _____ STATE _____ ZIP _____

DAYTIME TELEPHONE
_____

Quantity: _____ (x $9.95) = $ _____

CA residents add sales tax of 82¢ per book $ _____

Shipping $ _____

TOTAL $ _____

Shipping:
$2.50 for the first book and 75¢
for each additional book.

Send Check or Money Order to:
Walkabout Publications
P. O. Box 1299, Soquel, CA 95073
(408) 462-3370

Partial proceeds from the sale of this book will benefit the Advocates For Nisene Marks State Park.

Satisfaction Guaranteed or Your Money Back!

Walkabout Publications